C000008641

1 MONTH OF

FREE

READING

at

www.ForgottenBooks.com

By purchasing this book you are eligible for one month membership to ForgottenBooks.com, giving you unlimited access to our entire collection of over 1,000,000 titles via our web site and mobile apps.

To claim your free month visit: www.forgottenbooks.com/free192444

* Offer is valid for 45 days from date of purchase. Terms and conditions apply.

ISBN 978-0-266-19369-2
PIBN 10192444

This book is a reproduction of an important historical work. Forgotten Books uses state-of-the-art technology to digitally reconstruct the work, preserving the original format whilst repairing imperfections present in the aged copy. In rare cases, an imperfection in the original, such as a blemish or missing page, may be replicated in our edition. We do, however, repair the vast majority of imperfections successfully; any imperfections that remain are intentionally left to preserve the state of such historical works.

Forgotten Books is a registered trademark of FB &c Ltd.
Copyright © 2018 FB &c Ltd.
FB &c Ltd, Dalton House, 60 Windsor Avenue, London, SW19 2RR.
Company number 08720141. Registered in England and Wales.

For support please visit www.forgottenbooks.com

CLUB NATIONAL,

MONTREAL

7ᵀᴴ ANNUAL BANQUET

10th APRIL 1888 ,

SPEECH OF THE HONORALE HONORE MERCIER,

Premier of the Province of Quebec

F 5012
1888M 5

Mr President, Ladies and Gentlemen,

I sincerely congratulate the members of the National Club of Montreal upon the grand success of this, their seventh annual banquet ; that success proves their spirit of enterprise, their talent for organization and the ever increasing popularity of their association in our midst.

I thank you, Mr. President, for the kind words you have addressed to me ; they are too full of praise and I certainly do not deserve them ; I can accept them, I assure you, only as due to my colleagues in the Ministery and the Legislature and as applicable to those devoted and talented young men, who are to be found in thousands in your club and in other similar associations throughout the Province, and whose generous efforts have done so much for the success of our cause, especially in the two last elections for Missisquoi and L'Assomption, which terminated in two such signal victories ; I also accept this praise for all the true hearted men who have so well aided us in the battles of the last few years and whose wise patriotism directs and encourages us in all the difficulties of the strife.

I offer my thanks in my own name and in the name of the party to the members of Parliament and more particularly to those public men, coming from other provinces, who have honored us with their presence here to-night. We greet with respect all these distinguished men and we give a cordial welcome to these noble defenders of our political rights.

We all regret the absence of the Hon. Mr Blake, whom illness temparily keeps away from our country, and we fervently pray that he may soon return stronger than ever to renew his labours, continue his successes, and, in conjunction with our brilliant leader, Mr. Laurier, secure the triumph, at Ottawa, of the true interests of the Canadian people.

PREJUDICES

Before giving a sketch of what we have done since we have undertaken the management of public affairs, as well as of what we propose to do, it will not be perhaps inopportune to call attention to certain false notions industriously spread among the public by a certain section of the Press, for the purpose of injuring the Government, by arousing against it national and religious prejudices.

RELIGIOUS PREJUDICES.

The adherents of the Ministry are recuited for the greater part from the ranks of the Liberal party, the National Conservatives, who honor it with their support, forming, in the Legislature at least but a respectable and important mi-nority, whom we most highly esteem. Unable to urge against the Liberal party accusations which they consider plausible or which they would dare to avow, our opponents fall back upon religious questions and endeavor to evoke from the depths the spectre of Liberalism which has served them in such good stead as a political stock in trade in the past.

· I have, on several occasions, defined the political principles which I hold and which are held by all Liberals who give their support to the Government; but the malice and bad faith of certain adversaries who falsify true doctrines to attack and slander a large group of the friends of the Ministry, compel me to here reaffirm the political creed of the Liberals of the Province of Quebec.

DISTINCTIONS TO BE MADE.

There are two kinds of Liberalism : religious Liberalism and civil or political Liberalism. The Liberals of this Province repudiate religious Liberalism, which is condemned by the church, and hold to political Liberalism which is permitted. This Liberalism is justified in works published with the *imprimatur* [of the Roman authorities; it is of this Liberalism that, amongst other authors, speak the Revd. Father Ramière, a distinguished Jesuit, and Mgr Felix Cavagnis, now one of the most prominent theologians of Rome.

Allow me to cite these two Doctors of Divinity to give greater emphasis to the declaration which I think it right to make in order to remove all possible misunderstanding on this point.

·" There are Liberals, " says Father Ramière," who see in the standard, under " which they are enrolled, only its political color. Their Liberalism consists only " in the preference over absolute power which they consider right to give to other " forms of government that offer greater security to the liberty of the citizen.

" We do not write for this class of Liberals ; for never has Liberalism, " kept within these bounds, been the object of the slightest censure on the " part of the Church."

Mgr Cavaguis, formerly Professor at the Roman College and now the superior of that celebrated institution, it still more explicit. In his excellent work : *Notions de Droit public naturel et ecclésiastique*, published in 1880, which is a complete and methodical commentary on the remarkable Encyclical " Immortale Dei," this learned Professor treats most thoroughly of the question of Liberalism and this is what he teaches :

" Above all let us dispel· an ambiguity. " The adjective *Liberal* and the ·· substantive *Liberalism* are undefined, indeterminate expressions. They thereby " give rise to a confusion of ideas, become powerful weapons of combat and a " favorable means of propagating error. He who seeks for truth must first of all " remove all sources of ambiguity and misunderstanding.

" Liberalism has two meanings : the one good, the other bad. In the first it is " synonymous with being the friend of true liberty and not of license. From this " point of view, we are all Liberals ; no one likes to serve. Thus the word *Liberal* " would mean defender and propagator of the true liberty, civil and political, of a

" people without infringing on any right. This is a good and is being a Liberal of
" the olden time ....

" At N° 255 continues this author " we have said that Liberalism may be
" taken in two senses : one good, the other bad; now we may go further, specify
" and say that it may be divided into Liberalism, purely civil and into religious
" Liberalism.

" In a sense purely civil and apart from religious considerations, we call
" Liberal a person who is a lover of the civil and political liberty of his people and
" who seeks for it by means in themselves honest. He is consequently in favor of
" civil equality and political liberty, saving all rights legitimately acquired."

The remarkable work from which I have borrowed these quotations and
which I have brought with me from Rome, was submitted by the Roman Congre-
gations to the examination of the Jesuit Father Sanguinetti, a professor of canon
law of high authority, and that illustrious Doctor approved of it in its entirety.

I do not know of the existence in our Province, at least among the
followers of the present Government, of any other Liberalism than the civil or
political Liberalism of which Mgr Cavagnis declares himself an adherent. We
are therefore grossly slandered when we are accused of religious Liberalism, of
that Liberalism which is condemned by the Church.

To such slanderers I would recall the condemnation pronounced against
them by the great Pope, Leo XIII, in his Encyclical *Immortale Dei* :

" But, says the Supreme Pontiff, if it concerns purely political questions, the
" better forms of government, this or that system of civil administration, honest
" differences of opinion are permitted. Justice will not therefore allow it that men
" whose piety is otherwise well known and who are fully disposed to accept
" willingly the decisions of the Holy See, should be accused as if guilty of a crime
" because they may differ upon the points in question. It would be still a greater
" injustice to suspect their faith or to accuse them of betraying it, as we have had
" occasion more than once to regret."

There is in these words a valuable lesson upon which our opponents
should meditate and which shields us from the attacks which are prompted by
their bad faith alone.

And moreover I must declare that whilst favorable to political Liberalism moderate and confined within the limits laid down by the Doctors whom I have just cited, we respect and will know how to defend, if need be, those conservative principles which are necessary for the tranquillity of the State and the happiness of families, and we energetically repudiate all those dangerous doctrines which threaten social order, convulse conscience and society, expel God from the schools and only beget impious and revolutionary men.

I have often said and I will again repeat it to night, with the full assent of the Liberals who now surround me : that the victory of the 14th of October, 1886, was not a Liberal victory, but a National victory, and that the present Government, the legitimate consequence of that victory, has been, is still and shall, as long as I remain its leader, be a National Government, relying with confidence upon the honest men of both parties, vindicating the honor of the Province and defending its interests, healing the wounds inflicted on it by previous governments, forgetting the fratricidal contests of the past and seeking for the support of all men of good will, without distinction of race, party or religious belief, in order to consolidate our institutions and to prepare our country for the realization of the grand destiny which the near future opens out to our people.

RACE PREJUDICES.

The enemies of the National party predicted in 1886 that our triumph would be the ruin of the English speaking element ; if they were to be believed, we were, on attaining power, to abolish the Protestant religion, to interdict the use of the English language in the public schools, the Legislature and Courts of Justice, drive all the English out of this Province and confiscate their property just as was done in the past to the Acadians ; there were some, indeed, who went so far as to believe that we were to dethrone the Queen of England and to make war upon the King of Prussia.

These good souls must now be reassured ; we have now been in power more than a year and none of those dreadful things have happened, thank Heaven !

Queen Victoria is still upon the throne of England and not a single Nationalist, to my knowledge, has yet conspired with her European enemies to dethrone her. The King of Prussia is dead, I admit, but I beg of you to believe that the Nationalists of this Province are not at all to blame for an event which is a subject of mourning to the German race all over the world.

The English language is still spoken, with talent and success, in the Legislature and Courts of Justice ; Protestant churches and Protestant schools are still open ; in their churches distinguished ministers still eloquently preach the doctrines which constitute their religious belief, and in the schools Protestant children still learn to venerate the faith of their fathers and to love the glorious Queen who has reigned over us for the last fifty years, enshrined in the affections of 200 millions of subjects. We have here to-night seated around this table distinguished men of different races and creeds, who have come from all parts of Canada to testify by their presence to the intelligent harmony which reigns in our midst and to the desire which we all cherish to live in peace on this free soil of America, forgetful of the sanguinary battles of the past, and laboring, shoulder to shoulder, to create a great Canadian nationality. It has been reproached against me that when forming my Government, I dit not give a portfolio to an English Protestant ; those who thus reproach me are the very men who so well succeeded in fomenting prejudices, in the hearts of their coreligionists, as to persuade the electors of the Eastern Townships not to send a single member from their midst to support us in Parliament and those of Montreal West to reject the only Liberal Protestant whom the metropolis was in the habit of returning to Parliament.

Under such circumstances, we may well, it seems to me, characterize as hypocritical and fraudulent the jeremiads of certain Protestant newspapers, whose owners were more depressed by the loss of patronage of which our success deprived them than grieved at the pretended injustice done to those of their race. For it must not be forgotten that tho gentlemen of the *Gazette,* for instance, are more attached to their jobs than to their Protestant faith and that they would willingly sacrifice Luther, Calvin and even William of Orange in return for the fat contracts which Messrs Ross and Taillon were wont so generously to award them.

Let Protestants therefore relieve their minds : the Messrs White, of the *Gazette,* are the only Protestants whom our Government has as yet sacrificed and we do not propose to sacrifice any others. We desire on the contrary to continue to accord justice to all; we found that it was not just that the Protestant Chaplains of Prisons and Asylums should have a smaller stipend than that granted to Catholic Chaplains, therefore we put an end to the injustice which the Tory Governments had long continued to commit in that respect; we considered that we should keep faith with Protestants as with Catholics, and for that purpose the National Government returned to his Lordship, Bishop Bond, that distinguished man whom all respect' and to his associates, for the purpose of founding a Protestant Asylum, the Leduc Farm, which had been promised but which was never given to them by our Tory predecessors.

That property was originally valued at $10,000, and we paid over that sum as we had been authorized so to do by the Legislature ; but now that my friend and late colleague, Mr. McShane, has succeeded in obtaining $18,000 for it, we propose to hand over the difference to His Lordship, Bishop Bond, and his associates, and thus cooperate with them in the philanthropical work which they wish to carry out.

And if up to this, circumstances have prevented Protestants from occupying a satisfactory position in the Government, I may be allowed to say that those circumstances have changed and we will soon be enabled to render in this respect full justice to the English people of the Province, as we have already done in other respects each time that the occasion offered.

THE IRISH CATHOLICS.

A recent and regrettable incident, which entailed upon me the loss of a colleague whom I much esteem and who still remains my friend, despite all that may be said, may have caused my Irish Catholic fellow citizens to fear that their rights might be sacrificed in the future. This feeling is easily understood, but not warranted. I am the friend of the Irish Catholics, and always ready in the future as in the past to see that their rights shall be respected.

I defended them in the Legislature, when M. Taillon, in his subserviency to Sir John, was betraying then; I gave them their share of ministerial favors, while the Tories systematically ignored them ; 1 was the first to grant them a real representative in the Government of the Province; and if circumstances have modified their position for the present, I have reason to believe that before long they will again assume in the councils of the nation the place of which the voluntary resignation of Mr. McShane has temporarily deprived them.

The Irish Catholics! we are their natural allies as the Tories are their natural enemies, and in that grand old land of their forefathers, it is enough that an Irish Catholic should become a Tory to be denounced as a traitor.

THE NATIONAL CONSERVATIVES.

Our opponents bear us a most particular interest and, in their kindly solicitude, they loudly proclaim that divisions reign in our ranks, that the National Conservatives desire to abandon us, or that the Liberals want to get rid of them.

All this is pure fiction ; the Liberals respect the National Conservatives and the most perfect harmony reigns between all the members of the Ministry. We have the greatest esteem for the Honorable Messrs. Garneau and Duhamel, the two distinguished leaders in the Cabinet of that valiant band of Conservatives, who, hearkening only to the call of patriotism, broke all the ties of party and tendered us their hand in 1886, pledging themselves to work with us for the redemption of the Province. They have kept their work and we shall keep ours ; they bore the burden of the day, and it was but right that they should enjoy the reward : they have been loyal to us, and we have been and will remain loyal to them. They have rights as we have rights : now, as it is the first duty of the leader of a political party to respect the rights of all, the National Conservatives have nothing to fear, I will see that their rights shall be respected.

THE INTERPROVINCIAL CONFERENCE

The first article of the National programme, promulgated in 1886, was " the vigorous maintenance of the principle of Provincial autonomy against all infringements, direct or indirect. "

In order to follow up this article of our programme, we took the initiative towards the holding of the Interprovincial Conference, which met last autumn in the city of Quebec. Of the seven Provinces forming the Confederation, five were represented and I am happy to declare that the most cordial harmony constantly prevailed among the delegates. The understanding was complete ; all the resolutions relating to the proposed amendments to the Constitution were unanimously passed. These resolutions were ratified by large majorities in the Legislative Assemblies of Ontario and Nova Scotia and almost unanimously by that of New Brunswick ; they will be ratified by the Legislative Assembly of Quebec and by the Legislature of Manitoba, so that we can affirm without fear of contradiction that the labors of the Conference are approved by the immense majority of the Canadian people. The total population of Canada in 4,324,810 souls ; now, the five Provinces whose delegates have accepted the resolutions of the Conference, represent 4,110,014 of that total.

GENERAL OBSERVATIONS

Before entering into details concerning the labors of the Conference, permit me to call your attention to one fact which deserves to be noted.

When the National party was founded, it was contended that its existence would arouse against the Province of Quebec religious and national prejudices throughout the other parts of the Confederation ; we were taunted with isolating our Province and thus exposing it to the loss of all the influence, which it had and should have under the political system governing us since 1867.

Well, gentlemen, I would now ask you : what about this isolation of the Province of Quebec ? where is it to be seen ? where are those religious and national prejudices which were to arise in the other Provinces from the formation of our National Party ? Look at the labors of the Quebec Conference, examine its results and tell me, was there ever a time when our Province was more respected by the other sections of the Confederation ? Cast your eyes over the list of delegates who attended the Conference, called by the National Government of Quebec, and, tell me if the formation of the party which carried that Government into power really had as a result to arouse against us in the other provinces prejudices of race or religion ? Tell me has our Province ever enjoyed greater prestige, more influence ? We proclaimed our rights as men of spirit, and our conduct has been approved of and seconded by all true men, by all the real friends of Federal institutions in Canada. If comparisons were not odious, as says the proverb, I could easily show a contrast between the position we occupy in Canada under the National regime and that which we occupied under the administrations which have preceded us. The English speaking population is too jealous of its independence and of its liberty, not to despise men who would be so craven as to allow themselves to be crushed by usurpation or tyranny, and not to sympathize with us who have acted as citizens, proudly and energetically vindicating our rights.

All the delegates, distinguished men every one of them, departed full of admiration and enthusiasm for our Province and its people. Most of them were accompanied by their wives and with these ladies they met the elite of our society in those sympathetic social gatherings to which the farmer, the mechanic, the merchant and the professional man were invited, so that the delegates had an opportunlty of meeting the various classes of our society and of admiring their intelligence and politeness, and returned to their homes with a high and correct idea of our province, of its resources and its future.

CONTRADICTIONS OF THE TORY PRESS

It is an amusing pastime to read all that the Tory Press has published about the Conference. They commenced by representing if as a pic-nic, an unimportant meeting, a business which could only result in the discomfiture of those who had organized it. The more audacious did not hesitate to say that the Ministers from the other Provinces would not accept our invitation and would decline coming to Quebec.

Then were our worthy Blues in glee and jubilation !

But our invitation was cordially accepted by the Governments of all the great Provinces and then the jubilation of the Bleus sensibly diminished.

To keep up a little countenance, they fell back upon the uselessness of such a step ; but deception was again in store for them : the Boards of Trade of Toronto, Montreal and Quebec, composed of business men who are the most influential and wealthy men of those great commercial cities, addressed the Conference, even before its first meeting to obtain through it the assimilation of the laws respecting the liquidation of insolvent estates. This alone was a manifest proof of the usefulness of the Conference and completely demolished the silly carpings of the Bleu press.

Crushed once more on this score, these gentlemen gave up their sneering tones to throw themselves into wild outburst of fury, and on the very day of the meeting of the Conference, with the tact and delicacy, of which I leave to it the full responsibility and merit, the Montreal *Gazette* designated under the name of *Interprovincial Conspiracy* a meeting of delegates from the Governments of the five great Provinces of Canada. This way simply diappointment gone mad.

And yet its discomfiture was still not complete, for the newspaper, which then called us conspirators little dreamed that fifteen days later, it would be compelled to approve the greater portion of the result of that conspiracy. Indeed, on the 11th of November, the *Gazette* was obliged to eat its own words and to admit that the work of the Conference had been useful and fuitful, after having previously represented it as a ridiculous pic-nic. Allow me to quote its own words :

" Nevertheless, " it says, " it has dealt with certain questions within the legitimate scope of a Provincial Conference, such as the abolition of Legislative Councils, the confirmation of the powers exercised by the Legislatures since Confederation and in regard to which doubts have arisen, and the question of the boundaries of Ontario and Quebec. These are all important questions upon which the Legislature, at the instigation of the Conference, can pertinently pronounce and with respect to which there may be advantageous legislation for the people."

If we did conspire, at all events, it must be frankly admitted that we conspired for the good of the people ; even the *Gazette* has confessed this.

But let us continue the quotation :

" Many of the resolutions relate to matters remotely connected with the
" principles of the constitution and the free working of the Federal system, and as to
" which an agreement can easily be reached without disturbing the foundations of the

" Federation. In this class, it seems to us, fall the resolutions beating on the subject
" of the appointment of magistrates by the provincial authorities, the receipt by the
" provinces of fees paid on legal proceedings in the provincial courts, the power af
" lieutenant-governors to issue commissions to hold courts, the abolition of Legis-
" lative Councils and the ownership of Indian lands by the provinces in which
" they are situate, although this last question may be settled possibly by appeal to
" the Judicial Committee of the Privy Council by a decision based on the B. N. A.
" act. The power of pardon of persons convicted of an offence against provincial
" laws is now exercised by the Provincial authorities, but if any doubt as to the
" jurisdiction exists, it may well be removed, and the desirability of determining
" and establishing the boundaries of Ontario and Quebec will be generally recog-
" nized."

" These are all subjects, albeit of no grave moment, that may be advanta-
" geously settled by mutual agreement between the Federal and Provincial
" authorities, without disturbing the fundamental principles of the constitution,
" impairing the proper jurisdiction of the Parliament of Canada, or displacing the
" machinery of government."

There can be no doubt, and in this we agree with the *Gazette*, that many
of these questions might be settled by an understanding between the Federal Government and the Provinces ; but as the Federal Government has always refused
to come to such understanding, we were constrained to adopt means to attain
our ends without its concurrence.

Allow me to quote also the testimony of another Tory newspaper, one of
the most hostile and unjust towards us ; I refer to the " Star. " This is what it said
on the 10th of November last, in publishing the resolutions of the Conference :

" They deal with subjects of great importance and are worthy the careful
" consideration of every public man and every journalist of the Dominion. Many
" of the conclusions arrived at by the Conference will provoke controversy, but
" there are some of its suggestions which will meet with the hearty approval of the
" great majority of thinking men. The principal matters treated of in the resolu-
" tions are disallowance, the constitution of the Senate and provincial subsidies.
" The establishment of a tribunal to pronounce upon the constitutionality of laws

" enacted by the Federal Parliament and the Local Legislatures would, we think,
" have the effect of making the wheels of the Confederation machine run more
" smoothly ;· such a tribunal would prevent many bitter and irritating disputes,
" and would settle such as might arise, speedily and effectually. " ·

This reluctant testimony amply atones for the attacks on us which the
calling of the Conference had evoked, even before its object and the character of its
work were known. When journals like the *Gazette* and *Star*, the known organs
of what is most unjust in the English Tory party, are obliged to pay such an
homage to our work, it must be admitted that the work of that Conference must
have been useful, fruitful and of a great advantage to the country.

There are only three points on which these journals are not willing to adopt
the conclusions arrived at by the Conference; these are the resolutions regarding
the Senate, the power of disavowal, and the readjustment of the Federal Subsidies.

THE SENATE

As to the Senate, we simply ask that half of that body be appointed by the
Provinces respectively and the other half by the Federal Government, but only for
a limited term. Such a system would secure to the Provinces a certain measure
of protection against the encroachments of the Federal power and would free that
Chamber of the partisan character which distinguishes it as at present constituted.

I can hardly see why the Bleus should oppose such a reform; in 1854
when the constitution of the old Legislative Council was modified, the Tory Press
pronounced in favor of an analogous system, but one that was more radical in character. · Thus, the Montreal *Gazette*, which was then as now the organ of the most
fanatical section of the Tory party, desired that the Legislative Councillors should
be elected by the Municipal Councils, that is, it desired that the composition of
the Legislative Council should be absolutely outside of the control of the Crown.
The resolutions of the Conference do not most certainly go that far, and if the
Gazette could be logical, it cannot do otherwise than approve what we propose.

THE LEGISLATIVE COUNCIL

The resolution relating to the Legislative Council reproduce the idea which I expressed on many previous occasions, more especially in 1883. I declared in the House that on principle I was favorable to the abolition of the Council, but that such a reform should not be effected until it was demanded by the people. That is precisely what is proposed by the Conference and if that amendment be adopted, the constitution of the Council will not be changed or its abolition effected except in accordance with an address from the Legislative Assembly, supported by at least two thirds of the people's representatives. The resolution of the Conference, it must not be forgotten, is permissive, not imperative, and consequently nothing obliges the Government or the Legislative Assembly to take any action in the matter, at least for the present.

VETO POWER

As the aim of the Conference was to find means to maintain intact the provincial antonomy, we naturally were concerned about the power of disavowing provincial laws, a power so unjustly exercised for the last few years by the Federal Government. Carried away by party spirit and the mania for centralization, the Ottawa Government, on many occasions too well known to need special mention here, has interfered with the action of the Provincial Legislatures, and encroached upon the domain of their jurisdiction, by disavowing laws passed by these Legislatures, though fully within the scope of their attributes, or by legislating on matters within the province of the Local Legislatures. It is undoubtedly true that on many points, for instance, the License Law, the Privy Council has checked those encroachments and has decided in favor of the Provinces ; but during all these law proceedings the Local Governments have lost considerable revenue, and it must therefore be apparent to all men of sense that it is a matter of the greatest importance to put an end to a state of things, which is so prejudicial to every interest and so dangerous to provincial automony.

In order to mislead public opinion and to prejudice it against the work of the Conference, the meaning of the resolutions relating to disavowals has been grossly misrepresented. All that we ask is that the power of disavowing provincial laws shall belong exclusively to the Imperial Government, as is the case, with laws passed by the Federal Parliament and as was done before Confederation with laws passed by the Parliament of Canada. This is the only way to protect the Provinces against the arbitrary interference of the Federal Government with the right which they have to legislate as they please on matters within the sphere of their jurisdiction, and which right they never intended to yield up to the Federal authorities when their Legislatures were created.

Moreover, it must not be forgotten that now we are only concerned with the right of veto to be exercised for the purpose of protecting the general interests of the Empire or of the Dominion, and not in the least with cases under Provincial laws which would be *ultra vires* or outside of the jurisdiction of the Legislatures. These cases, which are the most important, the most numerous, and which interest us the most, are, by another resolution, submitted to the decision of the Courts.

There could not be any serious question of leaving any longer this right of veto to the central power. Simple common sense teaches us, that, on this point, the Federal compact contains a fundamental error. The Provinces and the Dominion are two contracting parties in this compact, and each of them has its rights and duties, and should, if not desirous of violating the very basis of the contract, remain within the limits of its attributes. Now, who should decide if one of the parties is violating the articles of the contract ? Surely it must be a third party and not one of the parties themselves.

And yet to-day it is the Dominion which decides without appeal that the Provinces have violated the compact, and the Provinces have no means of reaching the Dominion, if it has been guilty of usurpation of power. Evidently this system is too absurd and too unjust to be any longer tolerated.

It is said that this power of disavowal is exercised in England upon the report of a third class clerk in the Colonial office. It may be so; but, in that case, the Federal authorities, whose laws are thus imperilled, are in duty bound to complain. Do they make any complaint ? No ! they are therefore content. Is there then anything astonishing in the fact that the Provinces should demand a change from a system under which they suffer to one under which the Dominion does not suffer ?

Moreover the right of disavowal is at the mercy of party interests and is subject to pressure of political passions, which are always unjust, because they are petty and narrow, in a colony. In England, the exercise of this power, is above all small and contemptible considerations and follows the slow, but dignified ordeal of European questions.

I may add that any question of religion, race or education, affecting or which might affect the rights of the French or Catholic minority, will be decided with more justice in London, even by a Tory Ministry, than at Ottawa, by an Orange Ministry.

One would be inclined to think that the Tories, who pretend to entertain the greatest respect for the Imperial authorities, would have gladly hailed this resolutions, which is in reality the greatest proof of esteem and confidence in the Imperial Government. The opposite has occurred : the very men who have been ever proclaiming their loyalty from the house top, in season and out of season, made it a crime on our part that we gave this mark of confidence to the Government of the Queen. We can from this form an opinion of the value of the much vaunted loyalty of these gentlemen. When it may serve the interests of their party, they swear by the authority of Her Majesty's Government, as they did in the matter of the New-Brunswick school question ; but when their party interests are in any way opposed thereto, they do not hesitate in the least to throw the Queen overboard and to represent her Ministers as fanatics, unjust, dangerous men, at whose hands French Canadians and Catholics need expect no justice, in fine, men who only seek for a propitious occasion to dispoil us of our politic liberties, conquered at the point of the sword. It was the same men, or rather the adherents of the same party, who, in 1849, under pretext of loyalty, made an attempt on the life of Lord Elgin, burned down the Parliament House and signed a manifesto in favor of the annexation of Canada to the United States.

PROVINCIAL SUBSIDY

The most important of the resolutions of the Conference is that which refers the readjustment of provincial subsidies. It is also the part which has provoked the 'most bitter criticisms on the part of the Bleu press. The inspirers of that press are so accustomed to regard the Federal Treasury, as their treasury, as a thing belonging to themselves, to the exclusion of all others, that they consider as a theft and a sacrilege any attempt to make the people participate in the treasures which constantly pour into the coffers of the Government at Ottawa. And after all, what is it that we ask ? We ask, and rightly, I think, that of the twenty five or twenty six millions of taxes received by the Federal Government, it should grant to the provinces sufficient to maintain their local institutions without obliging them to have recourse to direct taxation, which would give their death blow to the Provincial Legislatures and would be an irresistible and fatal step towards Legis-lative Union.

Here is what we ask :

The subsidies guaranteed to the Provinces by the Confederation Act are of two kinds : the specific subsidy for the maintenance of the Government and the Legislature and the *per capita* subsidy, based on the figure of the population as established by the census of 1861, for the provinces of Ontario and Quebec, and for the other provinces, on a figure determined by statute. All the change we propose is to triple the specific subsidy and to base the *per capita* subsidy on the figure of the population, not of 1861, but as established by each decennial census. For the province of Quebec, this change would be equivalent to an increase of $347,968.80, calculating on the basis of the census of 1881 and at 80 cents per head for the *per capita* subsidy. Calculated on the same basis as for the other provinces, the increase of the specific subsidy, for the maintenance of the Government and Legislature, would only amount to $140,000 a year for our Province ; but, owing to the necessity imposed on us to print our public documents in both languages, which occasions an increased expenditure that does not exist in the other provinces, we insisted on getting $10,000 more and succeeded in doing so, so that instead of obtaining under this head an augmentation of the subsidy only to the extent of $140,000, like Ontario, we shall have $150,000.

RESULTS OF THIS AUGMENTATION

· I need not tell you, gentlemen, that with this increase of the Dominion subsidy, the financial position of the province will be perfectly assured **for the** future and that with this new contingent of permanent receipts, we will be enabled through the liberal encouragement of education, agriculture, colonization and public works, to give to the progress of the province a fresh impetus calculated to uphold the rank we should occupy and to secure the influence we should wield in the Confederation.

The maintenance of our Provincial institutions will be permanently secured and we shall have no reason to fear a Legislative Union, which might bring on its train many grave embarrassments for our provincial finances, or direct taxation. It is here that lies the greatest danger to our local institutions and it is to avert this danger that we demand a readjustment of the Federal subsidy and our independence in money matters.

FINAL ARRANGEMENT

To give to all the Provinces a guarantee that the compact shall never be violated and that no parts of Confederation shall obtain special advantages to the detriment of others, and especially to secure Provincial autonomy above all attempt against it by means of special subsidies, we have enacted a resolution declaring " the amounts so to be paid and granted yearly by the Dominion to the Provinces respectively to be declared by Imperial enactment to be final and absolute, and not within the power of the Federal Parliament to alter, add to, or vary."

With such a law passed by the Imperial Parliament, we have nothing to fear for provincial autonomy ; the moment that our financial position shall be secured in a stable manner, in accordance with the legitimate wants or exigencies of the local legislatures, there shall no longer be any serious danger for the relative independence of the provinces, which, thus assured of a sufficient revenue, will easily find the means to defend themselves against the encroachments of the federal power.

This is well understood by the partisans of federal contralisation and legislative union ; this also explains why they so furiously oppose themselves to the readjustment of the federal subsidy. They will readily admit that the actual revenues of the Provinces are not sufficient for the legitimate wants of the Provinces ; but in place of agreeing to remedy this insufficiency by calling upon the Federal

Treasury, they demand that the Provincial Governments should impose direct taxation. The *Montreal Gazette* has formulated this programme in full terms every time that there was a question of the readjustment of the subsidy. Listen to what it said in 1883, when a proposition had been submitted to the Legislature of Quebec by the Mousseau Government :

" What, it seems to us, the Quebec Government ought to do, if economies sufficient to restore an equilibrium between revenue and expenditure cannot be effected, is to divest itself of some of the charges now devolving on it and place them upon the municipalities, as has been done in Ontario. A larger proportion of the cost of the adminisration of justice, of education and of the maintenance of charities and asylums should be defrayed by the municipalities. Sooner or later, that policy must of necessity be adopted, and the sooner the better for all concerned."

Is that clear enough ?

There, gentlemen, there is the whole policy of the tories to improve the position of our Provincial Governments, now become untenable. Direct taxation ! and nothing but direct taxation ! Bring them back to power and they will apply that favorite remedy, curing all ills and easing all purses. This draconian policy, they have already tapplied it to the Province of Quebec ; they have imposed a tax upon *exhibits*, a tax upon commercial corporations ; they wished to impose their notorious tax upon deeds and contracts, and they would probably have levied more taxes, if the national movement had not expelled them from power.

Well, on our part, we, Liberals, will not have this direct taxation ; we scorn this panacea of Blue politics and before we come to that, we will make use of every means which wise statesmanship can suggest. With what grace could we go, for instance, and extort each year a few dollars of a direct tax from the far- mer, when it is generally acknowledged that in place of giving, he must receive from the Government, in order to enable him to introduce, into his agricultural operations, the improvements now rendered necessary by the competition with the farmers of other Provinces and other countries ?

What chance will we have of bringing to the country a sound and profi- table immigration, if we were obliged to show to the emigrants the bugbear of direct taxation, which has already driven him from his own country? And our worthy workingmen, who can hardly supply the wants of their families, what would they say, or rather what would they do, if the tax gatherer were to attempt brutally to snatch from them as a direct tax a part of their earnings? What would they do? It is unfortunalty easy enough to answer : they would emigrate to the United States.

We must do the very opposite! make living easy and cheap, that is true statesmanship! now especially when political troubles, revolutions and wars drive the honest and peaceful farmer out of old Europe! now when the closing of manufactures in the New England States force our brethern in the United ¦States to regret their absent country and to long to return.

No! we shall have no direct taxation, no new imposts. Fortunately, we are not of that school of politics so much thought of by the Tories ; before having recourse to such extreme measures, we will take all possible means which common sense and patriotism suggest to us, to avoid such a misfortune, and it is for that reason that we wish to compel the Federal Treasury to return to the Provinces part of that which we have conceded to them and which we require.

You will now permit me to examine with you the position which I occupy with regard to this readjustment of the federal subsidy.

On this point, the Blue Doctors are much divided. Some claim that I have sacrified the interest of my Province, whilst others accuse me of having organized the pillage of the other Provinces for the benefit of Quebec. As you see, this is a grave case and that you may see what we must think of the whole matter, let me lay before you the text itself of the accusations made against me by both parties of the Blue camp.

Let us in the first place consider those who tax me with treason towards our Province.

The *Montreal Gasette* says that " the resolution adopted by the Conference " was evidently drawn up by the Ontario delagates, seeing that it does not propose " in the division of the subsidy any change as wished by Mr Mercier."

The. *Courrier de St. Hyacinthe* goes further: " This means in plain

" French, this paper cries out in a prophetic spirit, that the financial changes
" which will be made by Mr. Mercier's Convention shall be so made for the profit
" of Ontario and not of Quebec, which has received its share of the favors of the
" Ottawa Government. "

As you see, it is clear: I have cast myself with a trap and will lose all.

In Ontario, the Tory creed is altogether different ; it is not Quebec which
is going to suffer by the proposed arrangement, but the neighboring Province. This
opinion has been most emphatically expressed by Mr. Meredith, the leader of the
Tory Opposition in the Legislature of Ontario. Allow me to cite his own words :

" But what will be, he says, the effect of this resolution ? It will be this
that the provinces which are not able to pay for themselves, would, according to
the hon. gentlemen opposite, have their burden borne by the other provinces. It
is upon Ontario that the weight will fall, it is this province that will be the sufferer. "

This worthy Mr. Meredith, with a good faith which I do not envy him, even
accuses me of having played upon the hon. Mr. Mowat.

" My hon. friend opposite (Mr. Mowat), he adds, wanted glory and the
Premier (of Quebec) wanted hard cash. The Premier got the hard cash and the
Attorney General the glory. I never knew a case in which Mr. Mercier was ban-
krupt. Mr. Mercier said to the Attorney-General : " If you want one of these
great questions worked out, just come down to Quebec and give me the money and
all will go right. " Mr. Mercier got the money. "

But note, please, that it is not for me, that money, but for the Province
and the tax-payers.

You see now, it is quite clear, it is not I who have fallen into a trap, it is
the Province of Ontario.

But in truth, no one has fallen into a trap ; we met to transact business,
and we transacted our business as friends, as loyal, honorable men, and we have
laid the basis of an equitable arrangement, favorable to all the interested parties,
thanks to the intelligent concourse which our friends of Ontario and the other Province have given us.

But in any case, as you see, my case is a grave one, as I am the target for the shots of Toryism coming from Ontario and Quebec, coming down upon me from two differents quarters ; I do not complain, however, as those dishonest tactics display the singular bad faith of our common opponents.

If you add to all this the intervention of the *Minerve*, which has thrown itself into the fight to say that I have not the credit of the initiative in this matter of the Interprovincial conference and of the readjustment of the subsidy, but that the initiative belongs of right to Mr. Mousseau, you will say that the matter is becoming seriously complicated. As you see, I am guilty and I am not guilty ; it is me and it is not me who is the culprit.   Understand all that, if you can !

And finally, in 1882, I was, on this very subsidy question, furiously attacked by the *Gazette*, a Tory journal, and warmly defended against its attacks by the *Monde*, another Tory journal.   Now, tell me, after all this, whether the life of a public man is not full of vicissitudes and surprises.   This is what the *Monde* then said to its English ally :

" The question of the increase in the Federal subsidy is making its way in " public opinion. There is every reason to believe that the leaders of all parties are " agreed upon this point and it is easy to conceive how difficult it would be for the " central government not to acquiesce to a demand supported by the unanimous voice " of the people.   Mr. Mercier, being in favour of such a step, it cannot but be well " received by the liberals.

" We do not understand why the *Gazette* should, in this connection, charge so " strongly against Mr. Mercier. The subject seems to be a very bad one upon which " to attack Mr. Mercier who, in this matter, seems disposed to second with all his " strength the action of the Mousseau government.

" We see with pleasure the *Herald* taking sides with Mr. Mercier and re- " futing the objections raised by the *Gazette* against the views expressed by the " member for St Hyacinthe, on a subject upon which there should be no difference " of opinion in the Province of Quebec.

" For, supposing that the subsidies should be increased all along the line, " what will be the result for the country of this distribution of funds ? A part of

" the surplus, coming from excise and customs dues, which are paid the consumers,
" that is by everybody, will be indirectly reimbursed to the contributors. Would not
' this be one of the best methods of diminishing the public burdens, because
" with the money so obtained, the Local Governments will be enabled to establish
' an equilibrium in their respective budgets, all of them more or less heavily burd-
' ened, with the exception of that of Ontario. As stated by the *Herald*, the
" Ottawa Government pretends that it is anxious to diminish the taxation
" bearing down upon the people. Well, the population of this Province is
" threatened with direct taxation, and by an increase of the federal subsidy this
' calamity may be averted, without changing in anything the fiscal policy of the
' party in power.

" Nothing serious can be opposed to this view. We therefore trust that it
' will prevail in the Executive Council and in the Parliament of Ottawa. We
' have already made the remark that the United States before the war have given in
' this respect a good example which ought to be followed in the interests of all the
' Provinces and for the welfare of Confederation itself."

When these opinions were written, the *Monde* was as much Tory as it is
o-day, but it had at least intervals of intelligence and patriotism, during which it
was willing to render justice, even to a political opponent. I regret that now I
am deprived of the pleasure of paying it the same compliment.

At all events, these contradictions of the Blue politicians, their petty civil
vars, prove that in justice and equity we are right in demanding a readjustment of
he Federal subsidy. That is enough for us, and for my part, I concern myself
very little with those ridiculous criticisms or with insults inspired by disappoint-
nent and party exigencies.

At all events, I claim for the National Government the honor of having first
aken the initiative towards serious and practical means of putting an end to the
policy of centralization pursued by the Federal Government and to maintain the
ndependence of the Legislature, and of having so far carried that movement, as to
ast consternation among all the enemies of provincial rights and among the
partisans, secret and open, of Legislative Union. This is already a success of
which we may well be proud.

IMPERIAL FEDERATION

This is another project of the Tories aimed at destroying the self-government of the Provinces and to force us in a disguised form into Legislative Union.

I need not tell you that in Canada, it is Sir John A. Macdonald who is the soul and inspirator of this anti-provincial movement. Seeing the Provinces organizing themselves to resist the encroachments of the Federal authorities, he wish to thwart their efforts by shifting the question to another ground. Thoroughly convinced that popular sentiment here is opposed to him, he would destroy that sentiment by associating with himself in his projects the most influential public men of England. For, mark my words, it is in England that we must seek the centre of action where are prepared the plans which are destined to rob us of the institutions which we so justly cherish.

The partisans of Imperial Federation are becoming bolder every day They have just proclaimed their sentiments in a striking manner and they have succeeded in making of their dream a question of actual politics, through the nomination of the new Governor-General, who is an avowed advocate of Imperial Federation. In fact, Lord Stanley has given it to be understood that he comes to Canada with the fixed intention and the firm determination to secure the triumph of that cause. That is to say, that he is coming here like Lord Durham in 1839, to complete the work of national destruction begun by the author of the famous report, which is so well known to all. And, *La Minerve*, the French organ of the Tories, compleasantly reproduces the utterances of Lord Stanley in favor of Imperia Federation and seems to welcome him, especially because of the opinions expressed by him on that subject. The fiat has thus gone forth, and all the French and English Tories must be in favor Imperial Federation.

The situation is serious ; we are confronted with the greatest danger to which our political organization has ever yet been exposed ; we are to have a regime forced upon us, of which the consequences for us cannot be other than most disastrous. Down to the present, we have drawn our life from the colonia system ; now, we are to be compelled to assume, against our will, the responsibilities and perils of a sovereign State, which will not be our own—to expose ourselves to the vicissitudes of peace and of war between the great powers of the world, and to the rigorous exigencies of military service as it is practised in Europe; we are to be saddled with a political system which, by means of the draft, may scatter our sons from the ice of the Poles to the burning sands of the Sahara, an odious system that will condemn us to pay tribute of blood and money and tear from our arms the young manhood, who are the hope of our country and the consolation of our old age, to force them into distant and bloody wars which we can neither prevent nor stop.

We, Liberals and National Conservatives, are decidedly, energetically opposed to this change and the National party of the Province of Quebec does not want it. We will fight with all our strength against this machiavellian project, and if its promoters ever succeed in imposing it upon us, it will only be by force and by guile.

CONVERSION OF THE FLOATING DEBT

One of the articles of the programme upon which we ran the elections of October, 1886, promised "the immediate adoption of energetic and practical means, to improve the financial situation of the Province."

We have realized this portion of our programme, by converting the floating debt, into consolidated debt, we have raised the credit of the Province in addition to relieving the budget of a considerable sum, by reducing the rate of interest on a good for portion of that debt, which was contracted by our predecessors.

When we came into power, the amount of that debt, or the sum total of the debt then due and of the liabilities maturing at comparatively early date, came to more than three and a half millions, without counting the four millions of contested claims, which we refused to recognize, but of which unfortunately we will be obliged to pay a large amount. We could not count on the ordinary revenues of the province to discharge this enormous burthen of liabilities, as for several years the balance sheet of our ordinary operations had shown deficits running up into more than a million of dollars. It is very true that the Treasurer of the Ross Government had announced à surplus of receipts for the year 1886-7 ; but on the other hand, it must be believed that this prediction was only a work of imagination or an electoral trap, since the net result of that fiscal year is summed up in a deficit of over three hundred thousand dollars.

There was therefore no other adequate resource left but that of a loan, to enable us to honor the obligations of the Province and, to that end, the Legislature authorized us to borrow three millions and a half at a rate of interest not exceeding 4 per cent, for the purpose of paying off the debts or of carrying out the obligations contracted by our prodecessors.

There has been a good deal of talk about this loan, and, after all, its history is very simple.

Very naturally, we asked for tenders in order to secure for the Province the benefits of competition. The lowest tender received was that of Mr. James M. Nelson, of New-York, who offered to take our bonds at 94% firm and at $3\frac{1}{2}$%interest. This tender was accepted in preference to the others, because it was much more avantageous, and my honorable friend, the Treasurer of the Province, placed himself in communication with Mr. Nelson, to conclude the transaction. On the 16th August, a contract was passed stipulating that Mr. Nelson should take the bonds on the terms. I have just mentioned, and to guarantee the execution of this contract, he should deposit to the credit of the Government, in the *Chemical Bank*, at New-York, three millions and a half in securities of the United States Government or of the City of New-York, and this, before the 23rd August, with the privilege, to the Government, to take possession of these securities, in the event of the $3,290,000, proceeds of the loan at 94%, not being paid in cash upon delivery of the bonds of the Province.

For reasons which I will specify in a few moments, Mr. Nelson was unable to execute this contract and on the 3rd September, another was entered into, stipulating the same terms as to the price of the bonds, but substituting for the one previously agreed upon, a deposit of $100,000 in money, which was to be forfeited to the Government, if Mr. Nelson failed to pay over the price of the bonds within the ten days following the notice of the deposit of the debenture with the Chemical Bank.

These statements fully bear out the correctness of the declaration which I made lastfall at the Cavallo Hall. At that date, the contract existed as I have affirmed, and, if it was not carried out, it was because the stipulated deposit was not made; and that deposit was not made because the bargain was too favorable for the Province and because Mr. Nelson was not in a position to carry it out. We took every precaution that could be desired to do business seriously and safely ; we insisted upon a heavy deposit, much too heavy, especially in the first instance, and, if the affair did not succeed, it was not due to any fault of ours, but to circumstances with which it is right the public should be made acquainted.

The carrying out of a bargain, so favorable to the Province, was prevented by three principal facts :   .

1° The almost sudden deaths of Messrs. Ross and Cossitt, two of the wealthiest members of the Syndicate represented by Mr. Nelson, deaths which broke up the Syndicate and rendered it impossible for it to meet its engagements;

2° The sudden and unforeseen order issued by the Government of the United States to insurance companies, requiring them to substitute Federal bonds for the securities then forming their deposits, which occasioned an unexpected rise in the quotation of those bonds and put at a premium all securities of the American Government ;

3º The regrettable and malicious intervention of certain institutions and Political personages, hostile to the Government, who did all in their power to place obstacles on our way and to thwart the success of our negotiations.

No stone was left unturned by the Bleus to try to defeat our negotiations at New-York : depreciating the Province, representing in a false light the nature of our negotiations, treating us as dishonest and incapable, asserting that the loan was not needed and would be repudiated by the people, &c., such were some of the delicate and patriotic means to which our adversaries had recourse against us on that occasion.

Each time we went to New-York, the Bleu papers proclaimed that we had met with a fresh rebuff and not only mocked and turned us into ridicule, but insulted those with whom we were negotiating. Our adversaries even went so far as to have us followed to New-York, where a spy was set upon our movements, and they caused to be published fanciful reports of our doings in order to alarm public opinion and to turn the American capitalists against us.

To throw the enemies of the province off the scent and to defeat their disloyal manœuvres, we allowed it to go uncontradicted that we had resumed negotiations at New-York, and while a certain personage well known in-political spheres was patriotically giving himself a world of needless trouble to wreck our pretended attempts and was having it proclaimed through the Blue press that we were on the high road to be skinned by a Wall street Jew, we were secretly and swiftly making excellent arrangements with a powerful French institution, the Credit Lyonnais, and I left abruptly for Europe to complete those arrangements.

The doctors had advised me to go to Florida and I was about to leave for that place, when the rumors of war and the alarming reports touching the health of the Emperor and Crown Prince of Germany, induced me to take myself the contract to London, to have it ratified there without delay by the authorities of the Credit Lyonnais, to settle with them certain objections which their agent had reserved to them the right to make and the solution of which might be very difficult, if not impossible, through the medium of correspondence. I cabled my honorable colleague, M. Garneau, who had retained his passage at Havre, to wait for me in London, as I desired to avail myself of his knowledge, experience and business relations, in the settlement of so important a question.

By leaving suddenly and secretly, I made it impossible for the enemies of the Province to further hurt us, and while the personage, of whom I have already spoken, was scouring the streets of New York in search of my pretended Jew "Solomon, " as he was dubbed by the " Monde", and to ascertain my movements and proceedings, I was crossing the ocean to London where, within four days after my arrival, Mr. Garneau and myself closed the negotiations and placed our loan beyond the danger of the fluctuations which the death of the Emperor of Germany and ensuing complications were soon to produce on the market. Eight days afterwards, Mr. Shehyn received his first million, and on the first of the present month, he drew the balance, the three millions and a half being now placed to his credit in the banks of the Province.

I may conclude these details by stating that the services of Hon. Mr. Garneau were very valuable to me in London and that I was delighted with the loyal and honorable conduct of the Credit Lyonnais throughout the whole business, from beginning to end.

DETAILS OF THE LOAN

We, thus, sold our bonds to the Credit Lyonnais, one of the most respectable and powerful monetary institutions in the world. Our securities were taken at 99 and at 4 per cent interest. The ordinary charges, expenses of issue, stamps &c., reduced the proceeds to $3,377,500.00 payable in American gold, at New-York, which is equivalent to 96½ per 100.

This is by far the most advantageous transaction which the Province of Quebec has ever yet concluded. Our four 5 per cent loans only produced an average of 97.19 per 100 or $97.19 per $100. Our operation produced the same result, less 69 cents per hundred dollars, although the rate of interest was a fifth lower. To show a return equal to ours, our predecessors should have obtained from their 5 per cents about $115.00 per $100.00; but, instead of that, they only got $97.19.

Here, it seems to me, is an advantage which is not to be despised, and yet the Bleus are not content! But, why are they so exacting to-day, while they were formerly so easily satisfied, when their friends were committing such enormous financial blunders that we are now forced to convert their debts in order to save the Province from the consequences of their ruinous operations ?

COMPARISON WITH THE LOAN OF 1880

Now, to be more precise, let us compare our loan with that of 1880, negotiated in France by the Chapleau Government and represented by the Bleus as the most magnificent of financial operations.

That loan bears interest at 4½ per cent and was for $4,275,853.34. It only produced $3,772,717.00, or 88.23 per 100, that is Mr. Chapleau issued bonds of the Province to the amount of $4,275,853, and he received $503,136.00 less than the Province will have to re-imburse. In other words, Mr. Chapleau paid a ½ per cent of interest more than we are paying and yet obtained from his loan $8.27 per $100 less than we obtained for ours. Taking the relative par values of currencies, the proceeds of the Chapleau loan is equivalent to a par loan at 5.20 per 100 and ours to one at 4.20 per 100, which makes a difference of one fifth to our advantage.

Let us see what these differences represent in favor of our transaction !

At 88.23, the yield of the Chapleau loan, ours would only have realized $3,088,050, while in reality it has produced $3,377,500.00.

We have therefore gained for the province $289,450.00 on the proceeds of the loan.

At $4\frac{1}{2}$ per 100, the rate paid by the Chapleau Government, the interest on our loan would amount to $157,500 per annum, while, in point of fact, we are only paying $140,000. We have therefore gained on the rate of interest $17,500 a year, which makes $700,000 for the 40 years the loan has to run.

Let us now put these figures together and we get the following result :

Gained on the interest......... $700.000.00
Gained on the capital.......... 289,450.00
_____
Total gain............... $989,450.00

Our operation is therefore more advantageous by $989,450.00 to the Province than that of the Chapleau Government. It will be admitted that this is a sum worth picking up.

Nevertheless, the Bleu press lauded the Chapleau Government's loan to the skies. Here is what *La Minerve* said of it :

" We are now in a position to show that these reports are absolutely false and that the French loan, at the rate offered and accepted, has been an excellent financial operation.

"The province pays an annuity of 6 per cent, or 5 per cent for interest and 1 per cent for sinking fund, on a sum of £800,000 and the bankers with whom our Province has done business have paid, in francs, a sum which, according to the relative value of the moneys, represents exactly 98 per cent of the sum of £800,000

" It will thus be seen that, under every aspect, the negotiation of the loan at Paris has been a good stroke of business, without taking into account the indirect results which we have a right to expect from it.

" It should not be forgotten either that the loan could not have been effected in London at 98 before it had been accepted in Paris. It was solely the action of the Parisian bankers which induced the agents on the other side of the Channel to make their offer.

- " Another piece of information which we can give our readers and which cannot fail to inspire confidence in this financial operation of the Quebec Government, is that all the loan has been taken at 98½, 99, 99½ and 100, that is to say, that the whole of it has been taken up above the rate of issue."

Now, in the first place, let us note the falsity of the Bleu organ's affirmation. The Government did not obtain 98 per cent of the loan in question ; we know at present the truth on this head and the public documents establish that the real figure was 88.23. The amount of the issue was $4,275,853.34 ; that issue only produced $3,772,717.00, so that the Province lost $503,136, which reduces the proceeds of the operation to the figure I have just mentioned.

But, if the transaction of the Chapleau Government was such an excellent financial opération, as stated by *La Minerve,* how comes it that our loan, which will yield nearly a million more to the Province, is to-day cried down by the Bleus as a bad bargain ?

I ask, you, gentlemen, if it is possible to carry nonsense or impudence further.

An English newspaper of this city, which claims to be a commercial paper, has asked " why the Ministers have disposed of Quebec 4 per cents, at 96½ when the city of Toronto 4 per cent debentures command 99½ and the City of Montreal debentures within a fraction of par, when Dominion 3½ per cents are quoted in London at 103, and the Colony of Victoria sells £1,500,000 of 4 per cents at 108 ? "

In the first place, we have not sold at 96½ but at 99. This difference is important and we beg our adversaries to make a note of it.

Then, to this captious question of the Montreal *Gazette*, I might reply by another question. In 1885, Sir Leonard Tilley placed £4,000,000 sterling of Canada 4 per cents on the London market and only got for them 101.08 ; at the same date, the Victoria 4 per cents were quoted at from 102 to 104 on the same London mar_ ket : why did the Ottawa Ministers thus dispose of their 4 per cents at two or three points under the price commanded by the Victoria 4 per cents ?

Let those gentlemen reply !

Moreover, as regards the colony of Victoria, there is no possib'e parallel to be drawn, I regret to say, between its credit and that of Quebec in the money market. Apart from the fact that that Colony has already effected three large loans at 4 per cent, _and that its credit was solidly established at that rate, whilst ours was not, its resources and its revenues are infinitely greater than ours, without taking into account that its budget for the five years from 1883 to 1888 shows a sur_ plus of $2,271,738.96 of receipts, while ours reveals nothing but deficits, aggregating over a million of dollars, for the same space of time. Of the £33,119,164 sterling representing the total debt of Victoria, in June last, £25,404,847, or more than three fourths, have been spent in building railways which are the property of the Government and which brought to it during the fiscal year 1886-87 a net revenue of £1,088,945, or nearly enough to pay the interest on its whole debt, which in_ terest amounted in 1887 to £1,272,591. According to the *Statistical Abstract* for 1886, published by the Government of Canada, the revenue of Victoria is equal to $140.45 per head and that of our province only to $2.20.

Where is the man of sense who will pretend for a minute that a Province whose revenue is represented only by $2.20 per head, can borrow on the same terms as a quasi independent colony, whose revenue exceeds $140 per head ?

Naturally, the same reasoning applies to the cities of Montreal and Toronto, whose sources of revenue are more elastic than those of the Quebec Government. But even the city of Toronto did not succeed as well as we did in placing its 4 per cents. It is perfectly true that it put them on the market at 99 $\frac{1}{2}$; but I have it from a most reliable source that it did not realize, at least for its own benefit, more than 95 or 95$\frac{1}{2}$, whilst we obtained 96$\frac{1}{2}$.]

But, even supposing that we did not effect our loan on the same terms as the opulent and prosperous colony of Victoria or the cities of Montreal and Toronto, what does it signify ? The great question is to ascertain whether we got the worth of our bonds. The securities of a government, like all other merchandize, sell for what they are worth in the market ; now, what were the bonds of the Province of Quebec worth in London when our loan was issued ? On the 3rd January, our 5 per cents were quoted at from 111 to 113, giving an average of 112. Now, at 112, 5 per cents are equivalent to par at 4.25 per cent interest. On the same date, our $4\frac{1}{2}$ per cents were quoted at from 105 to 107, giving an average of 106. But, $4\frac{1}{2}$, per cents at 106 are equivalent to 4.25 per cent at par. Lastly, 4 per cents at $96\frac{1}{2}$ which is the figure we obtained from the Credit Lyonnais, are equi. valent to about 4.16 % at par, that is to say, that we effected our loan on terms which give a larger return than the current value of the bonds of the other loans of the Province, when the operation took place, though it is well known that, to negotiate new bonds, it is necessary that they should present advantages over the previous issues, as otherwise nobody would have an interest in purchasing the new securities.

These considerations, which must strike all business men, clearly show that our transaction was an advantageous one for the province and that we got for our bonds not only the full amount, but even more than the full amount of their current value.

The paper of Mr. White, a future Finance Minister, it appears, has reproached us for having sold the whole loan to the Credit Lyonnais.

If my memory be good, that paper did not make the same reproach in 1876 to Hon. Mr. Church, when he sold the whole of his loan to the Merchants" Bank. In 1883, Mr. Wurtele sold the last £500,000 sterling of the loan of 1882 to the Bank of Montreal and yet the *Gazette* did not breathe a word on the subject. With what grace, then, does it assail us because we did the same thing in 1888 ? If the competition was advantageous in 1888, it should have been equally so in 1876, 1880 and 1883. Why did not the *Gazette* claim it to be then as it claims it to be now ?

Moreover, we created the competition by calling for tenders, which was not done in the case of the loan of 1880, that was sold directly and privately to Mr. Cahen, of Antwerp.

It is also a charge against us that, after taking the loan at 96½, the Credit Lyonnais placed it on the market or caused it to be quoted at 101¼ or 4¾ more than the price paid by it. But it has been forgotten that these 4¾ do not represent the real profit, seeing that the Credit Lyonnais bought firm and paid all the expenses of issue, of exchange, of stamps, etc., which expenses represented over 2 %.

Further, on referring to *Burdett's Official Intelligence*, I note that in 1883 the Bank of Montreal placed on the London market, at 107, the £500,000 of the 5 p. c. loan of 1882 which Mr. Wurtele had sold to it at 100. The *Gazette* and other Bleu papers, which are making a great outcry because the Credit Lyonnais appears to have made an honest profit, had not a word of blame, when the Bank of Montreal realized 7% absolutely in the same way.

Lastly, the *Gazette* seems to be very much put about because Messrs. Heidelbach, Ickelheimer & Co., bankers, of New York, appear to have been mixed up with the negotiation of our loan. Yet, it had not a word to say when the same bankers were mixed up with the loan of 1880; and I beg you to believe me when I state that, if they cost the province something in 1880, they cost it nothing in 1888, as we have not paid them a single cent.

Gentlemen, these remarks will give you a correct notion of the value of the criticisms which have been made of our loan, and I do not hesitate to say it is incontestably the best financial transaction which has ever been effected for the province of Quebec.

And yet we were in an exceptionally difficult position. Over and above the discredit resulting from the bad state in which were the finances of the province, when we undertook their management, we had to stem the current, or, if you prefer, undo the quotations established by our predecessors. After having first borrowed at 5 % and at a considerable discount, these gentlemen had come down to 4½ % in 1880, by sacrificing under the guise of a discount $503,581, and finally had been forced to come back to 5 % in 1883 ; they had proceeded by half points, whilst we had to lower t e rate by a full point, to arrive at one bound at 4 %, a rate which they never succeeded in obtaining. It was reserved for my honorable friend, the Treasurer of the Province, whose experience, skill and honor in business matters have earned for him the highest reputation, it was reserved, I say, for the Hon. Mr. Shehyn, to place the Province of Quebec among the countries having the highest rank in the financial and business world. In presence of such a result, we have the right to proclaim that we have again built up the credit of the country and to claim the cooperation of all fellow citizens who do not allow themselves to be blinded by party spirit.

This success is the more remarkable that the *Standard*, one of the great London dailies, at the time of the issuing of our loan, contended that it could not be floated on the terms proposed and we would be compelled to accept less favorable conditions, if we wished to see it subscribed for on the English market.

I must moreover say that in France we had a most favorable and sympathetic reception ; we were treated as brothers and were given all the advantages which good will and the most sincere cordiality could afford.

REDUCTION OF EXPENSES.

We have also endeavored in another way to retrieve the financial situation. We have lessened the expenses and increased the revenues. For the financial year ending on the 30th of June last, the expenditure amounted to $3,283,697.78 ; for the current year, we have only asked for $3,000,829.60, or $282,868.78 less than the expenses paid under the budget of the Ross Government.

We have effected relatively large reductions in the staff of the public service, either in dispensing with certain employees, or in not replacing others who have died or in having their duties performed by other officers, without additional salary. Thus, Mr. Schiller, clerk of the peace at Montreal, who was in receipt of a salary of two thousand four hundred dollars, was not replaced. The duties of Mr. Huot, Clerk of the Crown in Chancery, have been entrusted to the Clerk of the Legislative Assembly, Mr. Delorme, who will receive but a small additional indemnity for the increase of work which he will have to perform. The successor of Mr. La_ chaine, who was in receipt of $1,400.00 per annum as Inspector of Cadastres, receives but from six to eight hundred dollars, which makes so much saved.   Mr. Richard, who had a salary of $1,400.00, was not replaced, nor Mr Fortin, who was in receipt of $1,200.00 . The same was done with regard to several other officers, deceased, resigned or dismissed and I can affirm on the whole that we have, effected considerable and important economies, not as considerable as we might have desired, but as considerable as circumstances permitted.

I could multiply instances of economy effected by the National Government; but those which I have just mentioned clearly show that we have not failed to put our programme into practice every time that opportunity offered. We will do more, as soon as the settlement of other more important and more pressing matters will permit us to modify the organization of the civil service and to carry out all the re-forms of which it is susceptible.

OLD PARLIAMENT BUILDINGS.

When we took office, the Province had on its hands a property which was costing it an annual rent of $4,444 and returning nothing : I allude to the old Parliament Buildings.   In looking up matters connected with this property, we were informed that the proprietors of the rent in question, basing their pretension on the interpretation of the law on the subject, were claiming an augmentation of the rent and arrears to a considerable amount, that is to say, all the difference between the Halifax pound currency and the pound sterling, making $955.45 a year and $19,109.20 for the twenty years elapsed snice Confederation.

As we could make no profitable use of the property, the rent being too high, and as we desired to avoid the difficulty resulting from the claim just mentioned, we handed back the property to the Ottawa Government.   As compen-sation, we gave them up at the same time the Sewell property, which was bring-ing us in nothing and threatened even to become a source of expense, and we also transferred to them the proceeds of the insurance on the old Parliament Buildings, which were destroyed by fire in 1883.

By this transaction, we freed ourselves from a perpetual rent represented by a capital of about $100,000, as well as from a claim involving nearly $20,000, without taking into account that our action will also probably favor the carrying out of projects contributing to the development and embellishment of our old Provincial capital.

THE TAX ON COMMERCIAL CORPORATIONS.

In 1882, the Chapleau Government imposed a special and direct tax on Banks, Insurance Companies, Railways and other bodies. The corporations concerned refused to pay and a great number of suits were taken out and pleaded before the Courts, incurring considerable costs which had already, on our coming into power, reached a sum of nearly $50,000. These suits, carried in appeal to the Privy Council, in England, had been suspended in 1886, the year of the general elections : it is easy to surmise the reason. It was our duty to bring the matter to an end ; we therefore, as early as the month of April, instructed Mr. Geoffrion to go to England and to press the suits with all despatch. Mr. Geoffrion brilliantly succeeded and secured judgment in favor of the Government.

The collection of the tax was speedily made, and at the present moment we have received more than half a million of dollars from that source. Corporations which, after that final judgment, refused to pay, have been sued and must pay, for they can no longer escape condemnation. We apply this law, because it is the law ; but we believe that, in its application, it inflicts certain injustices which will soon be made to disappear, as well in the interest of the companies as in that of the Province. And if our plans with reference to the readjustment of the federal subsidy, as accepted by the Interprovincial Conference, succeed, as we have reason to hope, the Treasury of the Province will then be in a favorable enough condition to permit the Government to consider the opportunity of doing away altogether with this tax.

CROWN LANDS

Up to this, we were principally concerned about increasing the revenue. Thanks to the changes which we have made in the regulations respecting woods and forests, we have increased by almost $50,000.00 per annum the receipts arising from ground rents and by $100,000 those arising from timber dues. We have organized a system of inspection which will enable us to prevent the frauds that were formerly committed in the cutting of lumber on the Crown Lands and which caused every year a loss to the Treasury of considerable sums of money. We have in our possession the proof that in several sections of the Province, lumber merchants, the favorites of former Governments, have plundered hundreds of square miles of our finest forests. For the few thousand dollars which these gentlemen were wont to subscribe to the electoral fund or other assistance of the same nature, which they would give to the Government, preceding Ministries handed over to them to despoil the finest domains of the State. Thanks to the measures taken by us, these depredations will be no longer committed, or at any rate, the pillagers well be denounced and severely punished. We shall deal with the lumber thieves as we do with the colonization money thieves.

LICENSE LAWS.

We have devoted particular attention to the faithful observance of the License Laws, and the consequence of the reforms which we have therein effected will be seen in the very perceptible increase of the revenue coming from that source and in the more severe enforcing of the law. We will not stop there; we propose to submit to Parliament, at its next session, important amendments to the License Law, whose application will result in considerably diminishing the sale of intoxicating ·liquors and in punishing those who are guilty of violating the law. We have every reason to believe that the religious and civil authorities and temperance societies to which these amendments will be shortly submitted, will be fully satisfied with our exertions on behalf of the great and holy cause of temperance.

THE EQUILIBRIUM OF THE FINANCES RESTORED.

We have also brought to a successful issue several matters which are not without importance, and, thanks to a firm and vigorous policy, as well in respect of economy in the expenditure as under the head of the collection of the revenues, we have put an end to the reign of deficits and inaugurated that of *surpluses*, the figure of which this year will be very considerable.

CODIFICATION.

Another work which we have terminated and which should entitle us to the gratitude of the public, is the Codification of the Statutes. This work, begun in 1876, had been dragging on for the last twelve years. In taking charge of the Crown Law department, I resolved to put an end to these delays, which were occasioning considerable expense ; I procured from the Legislature the necessary authority to push on the work with energy; I devoted to it my summer holidays, and to night I have the satisfaction of being able to announce to you that the proclamation putting in force the *Revised Statutes of the Province of Quebec* will be out in a few days. I was enabled to bring this work to a close, thanks to the valuable and intelligent assistance I received from several distinguished colleagues, chosen without distinction of party, amongst members of the legal profession who gave us the benefit of their experience and their knowledge and have thus linked their names with the greatest legislative work of the province.

THE ASYLUMS COMMISSION.

The long disputed question of the lunatic asylums will also shortly receive a definite solution. In order to arrive at an acceptable result, we appointed a Commission for the purpose of suggesting the changes which should be made in the laws governing these institutions. This Commission, composed of men representing nearly all shades of opinion and offering all the guarantees necessary from the standpoint of principles and knowledge, have collected all the information desirable with regard to our lunatic asylums and the mode of treatment therein pursued ; they have visited the asylums of the province of Ontario, which are managed by men of the highest competency, together with certain institutions of the United States, which are considered the best managed, and I have every reason to believe that the report of this Commission will give us the necessary data for a wise and prudent legislation of a nature to satisfy all the interested parties.

AGRICULTURAL COMMISSION.

According to the unanimous recommendation of the Legislative

Assembly at its last session, we instructed a Commission to enquire into the means to be taken to improve our agricultural institutions and to reform, as far as possible, our system of cultivation. We considered it our duty to name without regard to political color as members of that Commission all the members of our Legislature competent to furnish us with useful information. For that purpose, we chose all the members who were agriculturists by occupation and who possessed a practical knowledge of agriculture, even those who were hostile to the Government. When it is a question of matters of such importance, so intimately connected with the progress of the country, political ties and party considerations ought to be set aside. The report of that Commission is now ready ; it is a most important report, and I am sure, will commend itself to the serious attention of the friends of agriculture. This report does honor to the intelligence and devotion of the members of that Commission, who under the presidency of Mr Bernatchez, member for Montmagny, have rendered a real service to the country.

The Commission specially visited our three agricultural schools and also a certain number of the most remarkable farms of the Province ; the members went to Guelph to see with their own eyes the magnificent agricultural college of Ontario, and they have prepared a report which will enable the Government to give a practical solution to that most important question, the improvement of agricultural education and of agriculture itself in our Province.

COURT HOUSES

We have completed the Court House at Quebec, and, on the 21st December last, it was opened to the public. This edifice has cost an enormous sum, but is very stately and comfortable.

We are now going to devote our attention to the Montreal Court House, for the enlargement of which we got a vote of $200,000 last session. Energetic and influential representations have been made looking to giving Montreal an edifice worthy of the great commercial metropolis and to be built on the old site of the Chateau Ramezay, opposite the City Hall. It is claimed that the actual Court House and the extensive piece of ground surrounding it can be sold to advantage and the proceeds would cover a large proportion of the cost of the new structure. We are going to study the question and consult the Bench and the Bar and come promptly to a decision favorable to the general interest.

In the meanwhile, I am happy to be able to state that the new organization of the Court House generally gives satisfaction to the public and that, thanks to the energy and supervision of the higher officials, the receipts are rapidly increasing, those of the last six months exceeding by $13,581 those of the corresponding six months of the previous year.

DEPARTMENT OF AGRICULTURE

To give effect to the recommendations of the Commission and to the law of last session on the subject, it is our intention shortly to establish a special Ministry of Agriculture and Colonization, and the Minister who will take charge of this new department, will be named before the 15th May next, the date fixed for the meeting of the Legislature.

THE NATIONAL PROGRAMME REALIZED

As you see, notwithstanding the illness which kept me away from the public business during several months, we have faithfully carried out our programme, as far as circumstances permitted, thanks to the industry and assiduity of my colleagues in the Ministry.

PROCEDURE LAWS

The length and extraordinary amount of costs in lawsuits require amendments to the laws of procedure.

We will endeavor to comply with this universal desire by simplifying the procedure in the Courts especially in commercial matters and by diminishing the expenses of litigation.

I sent sometime ago a circular to judges, advocates and to all whom I consider capable of giving information or of making suggestions upon the subject. As a general rule, it elicited replies and I have received very valuable suggestions, of which I have a clear and succinct synopsis which I will submit to the

Legislature, at the same time requesting it to adopt measures likely, to attain the
end so much desired by all.

As a first result, we will submit, I hope, a temporary measure which will
greatly simplify the collection of commercial claims, considerably diminish the
delays and cost of proceedings, and which, whilst we are waiting for a final reform
which is being prepared and which will touch upon the judiciary organization
itself, will afford general satisfaction to business men and to litigants throughout
the Province.

TOLL GATES AND BRIDGES.

The requirements of business and the necessity of obtaining easy communi-
cations will demand, before long, that a serious study should be made of the advisa-
bility of abolishing, in our Province, toll charges on roads and bridges, which form
real obstacles to free travel, so necessary to the progress of a country.

The solution of this great problem, so difficult now, may become possible
when our finances will permit it, thanks to the readjustment of the Federal subsidy
which the Interprovincial Conference has recommended.

COMMON SCHOOL FUND.

I hope we will soon settle, and in a final way, the accounts now pending be-
teen our Province and that of Ontario with regard to the common school fund.
Had it not been my poor state of health, which compelled me to absent myself from
the country for several months, that settlement would probably have been terminated before this, as we closed that which we had against the city of Montreal,
by which we received $125,000. But the matter is only deferred, and before
many months the Province will be in possession of what is due to it from that
quarter.

We have already received $100,000 on account; the Legislature of Ontario
during its last session, has passed a law to provide for a final setlement, and there
is now going on a correspondence between the two Governments with a view to

a definite understanding as to the appointment of Arbitrators, who are to decide finally this important question which has been pending for over thirty years.

THE QUEBEC FRONTIER.

We propose to give special attention to the question of the Quebec Frontier, and the Interprovincial Conference has already pronounced itself on the subject in favor of Quebec. All the explorations hitherto made clearly establish that the territory situated to the north of the Province of Quebec comprises vast extents of lands capable of colonization and varied sources of wealth. The lumber, mines and fisheries would offer an extensive field for industry, principally in the territory comprised between Lake Mistassini, James' Bay and Lake Abbitibi.

All this-country has been explored or visited by Father Albanel, of the so_ciety of Jesus, one of the members of that illustrious Order, which has contributed so much to spread the light of the Gospel and the benefits of civilization in all parts of the world. Father Albanel went through in 1672 to Hudson's Bay, by passing by way of Lake St. John and Lake Mistassini, and this is what he wrote to his superiors from the shores of that great inland sea :

"They have been quite mistaken who have thought that the climate is inhospitable either because of the great cold, ice and snow, or because of the absence of lumber suitable for building or firewood. They have not seen those vast and dense forests, those fine plains and grand prairies which border the rivers, in numerous places covered with all kinds of grasses suitable for the pasturage of cattle; I can affirm that on the fifteenth of June there were wild roses in bloom and fully as sweet smelling as at Quebec; the season there even seemed to be more advanced, and the air was mild and agreeable. There was no night, the evening twilight being scarcely ended when the dawn began to herald the rising sun."

This region, revealed to the world by one of the illustrious sons of Loyola, belongs to our Province. The accuracy of the information regarding it furnished by Father Albanel, has been confirmed by several English explorers, by Ellis and Robson, among others, and more recently by Dr Bell, one of the most eminent members of the Geological Survey of Canada. Like Father Albanel, Dr Bell asserts that this region comprises great tracts adapted to profitable cultivation, immense, forests suitable tor working, different minerals of value, notably spathic iron deposits of inexhaustible richness.

This territory belongs to us : the decision obtained from the Privy Council in 1884 by my honorable friend, the Premier of Ontario, relative to the Northern boundary of that province settles also, at least in principle, the question for the province of Quebec.

We propose to take advantage of this decision to add to our province a larger area than its actual superficies, that is to say, about 300,000 square miles. I have already brought up the question in the Quebec Legislature, in 1885, and a committee was named and instructed to study it ; we intend to profit by the work of that committee as well as by the Privy Council's decision, to have the question settled in a final manner and in conformity with the rights and interests of the province. The province of Quebec is the rightful owner of the vast territory in question and is going to claim it.

NEW RAILWAY SUBSIDIES

The railway policy inaugurated by our predecessors in 1882, and in 1886, being incomplete and unfair, should be abandoned or completed. It was our own opinion that it involved too many interests and created too many vested rights to allow of its being abandoned without danger to the Province and without ruining certain companies. We have therefore decided to complete that policy, and in view of the additional resources placed at our disposal, to supply the omissions in it and to repair the injustices which it committed. We shall endeavor to do justice to all righteous claims, without placing too heavy a burthen on the public treasury and, above all, without requiring new sacrifices from the taxpayers. We hope that our policy, on this head, will meet with the approval of all right-thinking men and largely contribute to the true progress of the country.

JESUITS' ESTATES

The final settlement of the question of the Jesuits' Estates has been frequently demanded by the religious authority : during the last twenty years ou predecessors, who had on several occasions promised to effect the settlement, never did so for reasons quite easily understood. We believe that the time has come to finish with this eternal question and we have decided to take it up and attempt to give it a practical solution calculated to remove serious causes of uneasiness.

We are not deceiving ourselves as to the number and importance of the difficulties which the solution of this question presents; but we think that public opinion demands that, by an equitable arrangement with the interested parties, the permanent causes of trouble which the actual state of things has entailed should be removed.

As yet, nothing has been decided as to the mode of settlement, except that the principle of the restitution has been abandoned by those concerned and that of a reasonable compensation substituted for it. In the meantime, we intend to proceed to the sale of the ground of the old Jesuits' College at Quebec, which, as every one knows, has been for years past in a condition to disgrace a civilized city. Hon. Mr. Chapleau, we are assured, offered in 1880 to pay the religious authorities $100,000 for this ground, but the offer was not accepted, for reasons which will be divulged later.

We are happy to be able to announce that there is no longer any ob_jection to the sale of this ground and that we are going to effect it shortly. The proceeds will be considered a special deposit in the hands of the Government, who will collect the interest until the final settlement. It is needless to say that this settlement cannot be made without according to the Protestant minority of the pro_vince a legitimate compensation, proportioned to their share of sacrifice in this connection.

CONVERSION OF THE FUNDED DEBT.

I availed myself of my trip to Europe and of the good dispositions which l met with in regard to the Province, to open business relations with two of the largest monetary institutions of France: the Credit Lyonnais and the Banque de Paris et des Pays Bas. After hearing the report which I made to them of my projects, these two institutions signified their willingness to undertake the conversion of the funded debt of the province, for the purpose of reducing and rendering uniform the rate of interest.

The first question put to me was a question of law : I was asked if this conversion was legally possible ?   I submitted the question to eminent lawyers of Paris and it will shortly be submitted to some of the first lawyers of London.   I have no doubt about the answer which those jurisconsults will give ; I have already in my possession the result of a preliminary study which gives a favorable solution to the problem.   There is a precedent : the Empire of Brazil effected two years ago, in France, and with all desirable success, the conversion of its debt, which was precisely in circumstances identical with our own, from a legal and pecuniary point of view.

Moreover it is a principle of international law that delays are alway supposed to be in favor of the debtor and the latter çan always free himself by paying by anticipation the amount of his debt.   This principle is laid down by article 1091 of our Code, which is but the reproduction of the Code Napoléon.   This article says that " the term is always presumed to be stipulated in favor of the debtor, unless it results from the stipulation or the circumstances that it has also been agreed upon in favor of the creditor ?

This is also the doctrine held by all the political economists who have written upon the matter and it has been put in practice by many of the Governments of Europe.   Rambaud, in his work *Du Placement des Capitaux*, clearly lays down the doctrine : " The right possessed by the State, says he, to reduce the interest upon its debts, by offering to its holders the reimbursement of the capital, if they refuse to convert it, is formally sanctioned by article 1911 of the Civil Code under the terms of which all perpetual constituted rents are essentially redeemable, the parties only having the right to stipulate that the payment shall not take place before ten years.   It is in consequence of this right that England successively converted its debt from five per cents to four per cents, and then to three per cents. In France, we have had successively the conversions of 1825, 1852 and 1862."

Mr. Leroy-Beaulieu, member of the Institute and professor of political economy at the Collège de France, where he succeeded to the chair of Mr. Emile Chevalier, lays down the same doctrine. This is what I find in his *Précis d'econo-mie politique*, published this very year :

" There is however one circumstance which from time to time comes to the
" -help of the State and which enables its statesmen to effect the conversion of the
" public debts. We have seen that the rate of interest has in general a tendency to
" lower itself in prosperous countries. Moreover, most nations borrow especially
" in moments of crisis, when the rate of interest is high, during or after great wars.
" France, for instance, on the morrow of its disasters, in 1871 and 1872, issued
" 5 % loan at 81 or 82 francs, so that for 81 or 82 francs the subscriber secured for
" himself a revenue of 5 francs, which represented in reality about six per cent
" interest upon his investment. A few years afterwards, prosperity being
" reestablished, the State could find money at 4 or $4\frac{1}{2}$ % interest. Taking advantage
" of this favorable circumstance, it could again apply to its creditors and propose
" to pay them back, at 100 francs, that is at par, or to reduce the interest to $4\frac{1}{2}$ or 4
" per cent. Such a transaction is perfecfly legitimate. This conversion is an option
" offered to the creditor between reimbursement of his debt and a diminishing of-
" interest. It resembles what would be done by a private individual, who having
" borrowed during hard times, 1,000 francs at 5 or 6 per cent interest, and seeing
" good times returning, would offer to his creditor to return to him the 1000 francs,
" unless he would consent to no longer require more than 4 or $4\frac{1}{2}$ per cent. The
" right of conversion depends, moreover, in France, upon that provision of our law
" which establishes that, except when otherwise stipulated, every perpetual rent
" shall be reimbursable in consideration of the payment of twenty times the
" amount of the interest.

" States are bound, in the interest of their citizens, to have recourse to these
" conversions, every time that their credit has sufficiently improved to permit of
" such transactions. It was in that way that the United States of America acted,
" when they successively converted almost all their debt, so much so that they
" now pay no more than 3 per cent interest, in place of 6 per cent which was the
" original rate at which they borrowed."

England at this very moment is engaged in effecting the conversion of £150,000,000 sterling of its public debt. The project laid before Parliament by the Chancellor of the Exchequer, Sir Henry Goschen, applies to three classes of three per cents; the consols the reduced three per cents and the new three per cents. The holders of the last mentioned funds, which are redeemable since 1874, will have the alternative of conversion or of reimbursement; if they do not make known their dissent within a certain delay, at the Bank of England or the Bank of Ireland, they will receive in return for their old three per cents others of an equal amount, for the issue of which the Chancellor is now seeking authority from Parliament. These new bonds will bear interest at 3 % for the year ending the 5th of April 1889, at 2¾ % for the fourteen years ending on the 5th of April 1903 and after that, at 2½ %. The bill stipulates that these bonds cannot be redeemed before 35 years, that is before the 5th of April 1923. Naturally they who will not accept this conversion will be reimbursed at par.

As to the consols and the reduced 3 per cents, the holders of these funds, who accept of conversion, will receive a dividend of 15 shillings per £100, payable before the 5th of April next. To hasten the conversion of these bonds, there will be granted a premium or bonus of 5 shillings per £100, to every holder who returns them to the Government for conversion.

As you see, the project of Sir Henry Goschen is the final conversion of 150 or 155 million pounds sterling from 3 % to 2½ %.

This transaction will greatly favor the one which we have in view and for which I have made the preliminary arrangements during my trip in Europe. No time could be more favorable for the execution of our plan. It is a business matter which concerns the best interests of the Province, a matter upon which both parties should be in accord, where there cannot reasonably be any question of political divisions, and I trust that the opponents of the Government will have enough of patriotism to cooperate with us in the accomplishment of an undertaking which is incontestably so advantageous to the country. It simply is a question of reducing the expenses of the Province by from $200,000 to $250,000 per annum, on interest account alone, according to the conditions under which the conversion will be made. We will be enabled to devote that sum to forwarding the progress of the country; this reduction of our expenditure will allow us to give a wonderful impetus to the three great principles of the progress of a country, education, agriculture and colonization.

The negotiations which we have begun involve the conversion of all our consolidated debt to a uniform and much lower rate than we are now paying. The Crédit Lyonnais and the Banque de Paris et des Pays-Bas, two of the most powerful monetary institutions of Europe, are disposed to undertake the operation, which will evidently be favored by the conversion of the English consols, of which I have just spoken. The greater number of English and other capitalists will perhaps believe it to be to their advantage to take our $3\frac{1}{2}$ per cents in preference to the $2\frac{1}{2}$ per cents of the Imperial Government, in order to gain one per cent upon the investments, and to increase by that much their income. We wish to take advantage of this exceptional circumstance and for this purpose we rely upon the loyal coo-peration of all the true friends of the Province. Our consolidated debt, including the last loan, is $22,354,353, 34: a reduction of 1 % on the amount of interest payable on that sum represents $223,543,53, which will be so much the less we will have to pay annually on interest account. And I have every reason to think that the reduction will reach a quarter of a million and even more, for there is no reason to prevent us from trying $3\frac{3}{4}$ and even $3\frac{1}{2}$ per cents, especially if the Legislature, hearkening to the voice of patriotism, vote for this measure as a measure of urgency and unanimously as it will be their duty, so as to give an additional strength to the negotiations which the Government will carry on in Europe.

I am glad to have this occasion to pay a public tribute of gratitude to Mr Dubail, the able Consul General of France in Canada, who, largely contributed to the success already obtained in the matter and who has generously volunteered his valuable assistance in the future negotiations, like a true friend of the province.

CONCLUSION

I must ask your pardon, Mr. President, Ladies and Gentlemen, for having inflicted so long a speech on you ; my excuse, if I can be allowed to offer one, lies in the importance and multiplicity of the questions I have had to treat and in the necessity under which I have been placed by the circumstances to give explanations on a large number of subjects that have of late keenly interested public opinion.

In concluding, let me call upon you, Liberals and National Conservatives to close your ranks and to unite like brothers for the defence of the common cause.

That cause is grand, noble and generous; you will have to defend it in Hochelaga, Missisquoi, Shefford, Laval and Maskinongé. Rally then like men of spirit around the national banner and ensure its triumph, together with that of the sacred cause of the country.

Lightning Source UK Ltd.
Milton Keynes UK
UKHW012324120119
335431UK00006B/426/P